T0363732

Mystic

By the same Author

Boozer of Blue 1990
Journey to Anima 2000

Mystic

Peter Eason

**Wakefield
Press**

Wakefield Press
1 The Parade West
Kent Town
South Australia 5067
www.wakefieldpress.com.au

First published 2007

Copyright © Peter Eason, 2007

All rights reserved. This book is copyright. Apart from any fair dealing
for the purposes of private study, research, criticism or review, as
permitted under the Copyright Act, no part may be reproduced without
written permission. Enquiries should be addressed to the publisher.

Portrait of author (p. vii) by Annette Hassan entitled
This Morning I Went Out
Typeset by Clinton Ellicott, Wakefield Press
Printed and bound by Hyde Park Press, Adelaide

Publication of this book was aided by a grant from the
South Australian government through Arts South Australia

ISBN 978 1 86254 781 0

**Government
of South Australia**

Arts SA

To Sophie, Samantha and Felix

ACKNOWLEDGEMENTS

To Rob Johnson for his insightful editing and foreword.

To Herb Bogart, Mat James, Geoff Kemp, Jeanette Lindsay and Barbara Preston for suggestions and support.

To Marianne Long for help with and typing of the manuscript.

AUTOBIOGRAPHY

A child, I knew everything.
It was required of me,
To learn about nothing.
Throughout my life
I have learned much
About nothing.

The more I learn
About nothing,
The more certain I am
Of knowing everything.
Now you know everything;
About me.

CONTENTS

I put my tales of you into lasting songs.
The secret gushes out from my heart.
They come and ask me, "Tell me all your
meanings." I know not how to answer
them. I say, "Ah, who knows what they
mean!" They smile and go away in utter
scorn. And you sit there smiling.

Gitanjali   (102)
Rabindranath Tagore

FOREWORD

The title of Peter Eason's collection obviously prompts a question. What is it to be a mystic? If this question were asked with reference to a particular religious tradition – Christian, Hindu, Islamic or any other – a relatively easy answer might suggest itself. But Eason's poetry, while it alludes at times to different traditions, owes allegiance to none.

It is all the more significant for that. Typically, mystics have adhered more or less closely to a particular religion, whether Eastern or Western. We think of poets such as St John of the Cross and, among poets writing in English, Vaughn and Traherne. Sharing a familiar religious idiom with their readers, they could at least draw on it in their attempts to convey some intimation of experiences that essentially elude capture in words. No poet writing today could count on any such advantage and it is hardly surprising – for this among other reasons – that today's poetry scene is not one in which mystical poetry flourishes.

In Eason, however, we have a mystical poet whose loyalty is to his own experience and who writes in an idiom that is distinctive and contemporary. The nature of much of Eason's experience is memorably evoked in "The Dissolvings":

> I am
> A salt statue
> By a dark sea
> I hold aloft
> A flaming torch
> And wade into
> My psyche

The image of the dissoluble salt statue is maintained as the poem moves from the "I" of everyday consciousness to the deeper levels of the psyche to "Mystery" – a reality that transcends the limits of personal consciousness, as it does those of language, but it is nevertheless intimately present to it.

You could say, then, that to be a mystic, on Eason's understanding of the word, is to attach supreme value to experiences in which the habitual, largely socially constructed self falls away and a deeper, liberated, more inclusive self takes over – though once the constructed self falls away, the very concept of self obviously becomes problematical. No wonder that in "Plank" the self becomes scattered and dislocated.

Unsurprisingly, while this collection pays tribute to Christian mystics of the past – Meister Eckhart and Dame Julian of Norwich – there is no suggestion of Christianity's insistent differentiation of creator and creature, God and the individual soul. To that extent, Eason seems to have more in commmon with the Hindu philosophy that proclaims the essential identity of God, the universal self, and the individual self – a view summed up in its formula: "That art thou".

It is entirely in keeping with this sort of perspective that, in Eason's poetry, there is a recurrent transgressing of boundaries between humans and the natural world and between both and that (call it "God" if you wish) from which both derive their being. In the opening poem, "The Sensors Of The Stars", there is the contention that, in our wonder at the universe, the universe ("God") is becoming aware of itself.

From this point of view, the individual life is seen as no more (and no less) than a phase in the universal procession going back to cosmic and biological evolution, to the mystery from which everything derives. Death is an unravelling of what came together at birth, a return to where we have always belonged. This of course is not a perspective that can easily be maintained in the circumstances of ordinary life. It is the product of privileged moments. It is none the less heartening to recall such moments or to share in them. This is what Eason's collection enables us to do.

Rob Johnson

Throw your clothes and body away

THE SENSORS OF THE STARS

Obviously

The stars made eyes
So they could see

They made ears
So they could hear

So listen carefully
And see clearly

For the stars

COSMIC CLERK

The electric light shines
All over the cosmos
Lights shine
It's early morning
My mind drifts off for a break
And goes for a think
Around the block
Of the cosmic city
What incredible lights
What offices
Working through the night
What an amazing company
Invests in the sky
The expansion   the development
The long-term plan
My job is secure
My superannuation
Is perfectly safe
Still   I'm ambitious
For promotion   increments
And the Boss is everywhere
So I return to my work
Record what I am meant to
Report what I am able to
As a small   cosmic clerk

DID YOU SEE THAT BLOODY HORSE?

Five K's out of Andamooka
We drove on red
To the north emus strutted low bush
Where wild brumbies grazed
To the south   one horse
A big powerful grey
His right foreleg crooked
Stood metres from the track
Beyond him the country stretched
And seemed to radiate
To the vast pale sky
He stared at me
As we drove by
His unbroken face
Would haunt anyone not free
There was no doubt
His was the face of God
He wore the long serious smile
Which must belong to God
I want to know what it means
To wear that face
About ten K's on Mat asked suddenly
"Did you see that bloody horse?
He was staring at me"

NECESSARY TAUTOLOGY

When I'm out there
When I'm approaching
When I'm trekking
Through old questions
Across cinnamon
Into blue
When I'm fossicking
In the rubble   the sediment
Of ancient thought
When I glimpse You
In the traces of memory
The flecks of vision
Why do You elude me
Your presence everywhere
But You unfound

I return   lost
To catalogue evidence
The flecks   that transfix
The traces   that transport
And in the work
Again I seem
To close on You
Trekking out
Across cinnamon
Into blue
Words fossicking
Lines sifting
A poem   sometimes striking
In deepest vein and fold
Your Immanent Immanence

MYSTIC TO MARKET

Vulnerable?
Exposed?
A gardener who cultivates
What I grow
Must be
There is no cash crop
Mine must be
Cut in the mind
And pressed into poetry
With the scent
And flavour of ecstasy
You may transact
If narcotic enough
Transparent enough
For you to come through
Through to me
And we proceed
Back up a high road
I come with my essence
Where smooth grey terrace
And deep folded crevice
Broadcast   receive
The mystery seeds
And you conceive
Delivery

ILLUMINATION OR INFLATION

Naked
I knelt
And washed in the Passage
My hands
Two miles long
Scooped up the blue
And washed my face
My three mile face
My one mile brow
Pure blue spilled
From the hands
That washed the face
And another   stood up
Twenty   infinite miles high
And donned
The deep-piled black
And spangled robe

NUT AT SNAPPER POINT BEACON
KANGAROO ISLAND

Along the cliff I stormed
As agitated as the sea
At the beacon
I climbed blasted sky
Its smoke blowing east
Rain came
I descended
Sheltered   and stared
At the foundation
I watched ants
In the bevelled   channelled
Grey concrete joins
The concrete expanded
To a vast windy space
Where giant rain spots
Patterned my mind
I travelled with the ants
Across the rain stains
Around the simple geometry
Of flat   channelled spaces
Into the crevices
And fell down one so deep
It might have been mind
And look
I was content
And laughed
And became again
Significant
Became again
The sea   the sky
Ants   concrete
I studied a strut

A stainless steel bolt
And believe me
I saw everything
Look at concrete runnels
And ants some time
Stare at a bolt
And imagine yourself
Standing under a beacon
Certain you are
A universal nut

AUTISM OR MYSTICISM

I hit a telephone pole
And it rang back
Standing in a paddock
Hitting a pole with a stick
It rang back
Standing and listening
To the instant
And sharp echo-crack
Of a pole and stick
I stand back
Watch the swinging
Hear something else
In the sharp echo-crack

I have struck so long
The poles of being
That I hear echoing
The silent ringing
Of my becoming
From no beginning
And I swing forward
As I swing back

AS ONE GUISE OR ANOTHER

I was greeted by
An ecstatic, slack jawed
Paper dispenser,
Its sodden torn tongue
Lolling into a bashed basin.

The urinal stretched the room,
But despite its stench
It had a presence,
Like a moat and wall,
Or a silent fall.

The cubicle had no door,
And the pan was seatless,
Stained and encrusted,
But sat unmoved,
Solitary, serene,
Like a pagan shrine,
Or a deep, still mind.

The concrete floor,
Once dark sea-green,
Was stagnant and shallow,
As if evaporation had exposed
Its grey bed.
Around the edges though,
Through floating and congealed
Spittle and phlegm,
Pools of green were still deep
Under a lone electric sun,
Which shone a vomit-yellow pride
Through fly-spots and webs.

The place seemed strangely comfortable,
In a stoic, even devout way.
There was no shame.
Everything told me,
"We will be transformed,
Already Paint has evaporated
And Door and Seat oxidized."

And there was a consensus
That until act or accident or entropy,
They would remain uncomplaining
In their present state.
For, hadn't they been,
And wouldn't they be,
What are thought, "Higher" things?
"And aren't we all,"
They called after me
As I zipped and left,
"Shat, spat and pissed upon,
At one time, or another,
In one place, or another,
As one guise, or another?"

PLANK

There is a long plank
I'm standing at both ends
I'm shouting at myself
From both ends
All about are planks
On every one
I'm standing at both ends
I'm standing
And shouting at myself

The planks see-saw
I'm shouting at myself
From high ends
I'm shouting at myself
From low ends

They switch poles
And I'm shouting at myself
From foreign ends

They spin
And I don't know
How I'm standing
But I am
And I'm still shouting

All the while
In the middle
Of each plank
My voices mingle
Meld and balance
And I'm sitting
Sitting at the centre
Sitting
As someone
I never knew
Silent

BECOMING

They were flares

They were flames

They were flares
Of pollen and scent

They were flames
Of lichen and salt

They were flares
Of pollen and scent
Soaring on the cliff

They were flames
Of lichen and salt
Roaring on the coast

She was

She was the trees

She was the trees
The rocks

THIS MORNING I WENT OUT

This morning, I went out.
I went out past my chair,
Past my papers, radio, TV.
I went out past my walls.
I went out past my eyes, my ears,
Past my heart.
I went out past thoughts, dreams, visions,
Past ecology, wilderness, survival.
I went out past icons, religion, Gods.
I went out past light, dark,
Good, bad, all opposites.

This morning, I went out
To emptiness, silence.

I haven't moved.

THE DISSOLVINGS

I am
A salt statue
By a dark sea
I hold aloft
A flaming torch
And wade into
My psyche

My psyche
Is a salt statue
By a dark sea
It holds aloft
A flaming torch
And wades
Mystery

Mystery
Is a salt statue
By a dark sea
It holds aloft
A flaming torch
And wades back
Into me

THE SEAS OF OTHER WORLDS

The seas
Of other worlds
Make me smile
Their mountains
Make me climb
Their sharks
And carrion birds
Keep me cleansed
In cold silences
Below and above
And the mystic
Is home again

RAFT

The raft
Drifts ocean
And I am very thirsty
Sometimes
Like a sail
A breast appears
And presents to me
In the dark
Whether lover or mother
Or saviour
I never see
But the milk
Always
A draught
Of mystery

THE SHORES OF MYSTERY

Beaching my frail
And leaky raft of words

I comb for lines
Along those shores

Drift off   to log the draft
Unless sudden silent waves

Break up my little craft
And carry me into emptiness

BAPTISM

The farmer gave me
A bucket of water
I drank from my hands
Then plunging again
In the ascending cup
Attachment washed
From my eyes

I poured the bucketful
Over my head
Sudden light
Lit a limbed thing
Bathed in itself
Robed in itself
And shining

Shining

CLEARED

Felt something clear
– Some blocker of blood –
And in the sweet current
Freshened senses strained
To a perfected net
Trapping in the flooding
Light and air
Shoals of rainbow-health
And young happiness

ARCHE-POLOGIST

Mostly I specialise
In dreams drawn
In the cave of myself
The living hieroglyphs
Of wandering archetypes
Inhabiting me
I interpret them
In the field
And so far as I have
They compel me to
Forgive myself
For I know not
What I do

SOUNDS

What sound
Do cells make
As they divide
The blood
As it floods
What the zap
At synapse
The click
When a thought fits
What the roar
When concepts pour
And the pitch
Of the key
That opens up
The visionary

LOCATING OR DISSOCIATING

In the black plunge pool
After the sauna   the steam
I sank my senses
In the weightless dark
Crouched in a corner
I forgot my heart
In that sonar dark
I seemed pre-being
Aware   without breathing
A presence
Not beating

BLUE LADDER

I'm climbing a ladder
It's blue
Can't be seen
Goes straight up
Like those on silos
Or radio towers
I'm climbing through cloud
Below   forty-five years
Up   Don't know
But I'm climbing
And then rungs end
And at the top
Watching the universe
I see myself

I HEAR MY OWN HEART

I hear my own heart.
Sitting in my chair,
Staring down the Passage,
My ears fill
With my life's beat,
Its fleshy engine
Down-tempo of that ship's
Pomp-Pomp-Pomp
Across the calm.
I sit and stare,
And beat the journey.

2D SEA

Calcified
In sea-soils
Green and chalk
Slate and blue
Are small boats

On top a ship
Sits like a stone

THE LAMB AT NIGHT

Standing under a row
Of thrashing mallee
The rain crashing
Standing with the flock
On this first night
Bleating
The lamb hears
The bone-strewn paddocks
Flashing

EYE

Stand on eye
Out deep
Sunk in space
And dive

Submerged in vision
Bright and dim
Peer in or out
At everything

GULL

A gull
There in the wind
Lone   resolved   still
He glides up
Sensing perhaps
Partisan company
He seems so intent
Watching the sea
Now and then
He comments gratuitously
In clear and certain mews
I wonder if he's waiting
For a Messiah Gull
From a sea in the sky
Perhaps he has known
Perfect grace
And has become
The gull he wants to be
I wonder at our lives
In sandy proximity

Incommensurable

Obviously

ANTECHAMBER BAY SANDPIPERS

Often
Walking round the bay
Slate and turquoise
Lying out
Sliding round
Pipers divine
The sands ahead
They pipe on
To some prophecy
Then wing
At the mainland
They land behind
Pipe off
Exasperated
I won't see

I continue

Very stupid

Very pleased

EAGLE

In the light
Dust

On the pane
Web

Above the ocean
Eagle

On the pane
Web

In the light
Dust

ARCHETYPE

Across the Passage
Closing on cliffs
Lone in shaft-light
A white wave shifts

Deep in the psyche
Sea of all drift
Below reason
A twin ghost lifts

GRASSHOPPER

Grasshopper
It's a long hop
Since I saw you
Forty-five years

I saw you again today
Little hopping man
In the yellow grass
You are an amazing fact
An amazing fact
My child's mind
Saw you again
In the yellow grass
My man's mind found you
In grey grass
For the first time   again

Your conical eye
Followed my hand
What did you understand
What did you understand
Little man
What do I
What do I
Who loves you
Brown hopper
Brother in yellow grass
Brother in grey grass

I'm clearing all junk
Little brown man
In grey grass
I'm clearing it
To always see you
Little friend   little man
Watching from behind a blade
Watching   avoiding my hand
My gentle   child's hand

MULTICULTURAL FURNITURE

All my furniture is unrelated,
But accepted, as it were, like refugees
From second-hand stores
And domestic crises.
I don't discriminate.
I'm usually accepting
Of my displaced objects.
Individually, I sponsored each one.
I admitted them.
But because I dreamed a longing
For some integrated form,
Some unity, and authoritative style,
Today I feel inhospitable, intolerant.
I want to cleanse,
To establish a fundamental,
Final solution to being.
I'm not content with
The multiple treaties of my selves,
And decree monoculture
Is happier than the multiculture
Of my selves, and furniture.
For a fanatical hour I plot
To suppress and sell,
Purge and purify.
But I'm soon confronted
By urbane and casual questions,
Which examine credentials,
And arrest my dream-dialectic
And genocidal manifesto.
And as I begin to interrogate myself,
Remembering all things are really One,
The wary furniture settles calmly again,
Along with the nations of my mind.

HERO TO HARBOUR

Hero hissed 'cross slate
Glazed with lunar-wash
The starboard native winds'
Black feet were glaireous

The lone yacht was breathing
Dolphin quick star-white
Her symbiotic voices
Divining distant lights

And the glass ship singing
And slipping through the night
Was a single fibre
Of a single life

Sailing in itself
And waking the source
Steering cosmic ocean
By hermetic course

DISCOVERY

The Southern Ocean
A stretching water of months
Flooding sea and sky
Washing all green   every blue
Into eyes surveying
The low Southern Land

The Southern Ocean
An absorbed sea
Searching eternity south
Empty   save for impatient sails
And a slow hull
Flinders   in the vast breathing

The Southern Ocean
Blue-dark   blowing
Native dolphins smiled
"Discovery   is emptiness   mapless"
Canvas flapped full

The Southern Ocean
Mind spliced to emptiness
Flinders mapped the Southern Land
Transposed it   simply
For Western eyes

SCHOOLBOY ALCHEMIST

Sent out on a message
I returned through the sun
Past the rotting posts
Of an old wire fence
Where alluvial daisies
Stopped
And gave enough gold
To keep me
From the minor
The menial and meagre
And   for that matter
The major   the mighty
And magnificent
Forever

INFANT'S VISITORS

A glass of rainwater
As clear as me

A curtain's blue spots
Blowing through me

A little girl's mouth
Confiding to me

A grace that tells me
Peter   you are a good boy

You are a good boy   Peter

LOST LANGUAGE

Age six
From the dark throat
Of the wide passage
The breath of Schubert
Escapes the screen door's
Wrought-gothic mouths
And the mosaic verandah
Is a long chapel
Of wisteria light
Where I retrieve
My native language

OUT OF NOWHERE

Strange facts
Heads and hats
So out of nowhere
From where I watched
In my newness
I laughed amazed
At putting on
And taking off
Of grandma's
Wide black hat
The felt fibres
Hazing the rim
Her forehead's powdered
Lined blotched skin
Her white hair
Made me stare
Her head and hat
So out of nowhere
Head and hat
That they should be
Were two ways
Of mystery

RETURN TICKET

Suddenly happy
It is the yellow
Of the bus-stop pole
Over the grey
It has transported me
To childhood
Where I rode
Long distances
Into colour

ANIMA IN COMPOSITION

I'm tiling.
Diamond tiles.
A platform.
In the depths.
In the darkness.
The stars about.
Beneath,
The swirling grey
Of cerebral ferment.
A trowel in my hand
I set more diamonds.
And she sits,
Arms about knees,
Silently singing
A pattern of me.

TOO CLOSE TO OCEAN

They say she lives
Too close to ocean
They see the fish
Swimming in her
Hear the sea-birds
Crying from her
Feel a tide
Pulling them to her
Glimpse the moon
Gliding through her
"Move to town"
They tell her
"Get a persona
And have a living"
They advise her
They warn her

SHE GIVES THESE THINGS NO NAME

She gives these things no name
And nameless knows them better
Moon and sea now unnamed
Detach   and float before her

And written like a dream
Are forms   from which she reads
One of her own lost states
Of moon-on-sea

Eyes   name-closed   open
Mind   of names redeemed
She floats clear and nameless
With the unnamed moon and sea

SHE TELLS OF THE GRASS

He didn't know
But I was holding
The dune grass
While he made love to me

That's why I picked some
A few days later
While he was walking
Coming back

He saw me
In my T-shirt
Half naked
Gathering it

The vase arranged
He stared at the grass
Against the window
The window against blue

And he went from me
Staring at the grass
Reflecting the grass
Just grass

He reflected
Not defining
Like a mirror
And knew

He could
See grass
Anything
Any way

And when he saw this
He knew how
To re-enter
The Ocean

And only I could know
That he had merged
That he might
Never return

Only I could know
He was somehow
Everything everywhere
And might never emerge

And I thought
If he didn't
I'd wait forever
At his shore

Wait with the grass
In the blue window
For him
To restore

The grass
The dunes
The sea
The blue

Now that he enters them
As he enters me
Say I am them
And frighten me

CALL TO CAPE COUTTS

She calls
From train
Between Berlin
And Den Haag
"I love you,"
Silence
"Have you anything
To say to me?"
Silence
"I've only got
A few coins left …"
The line goes dead
She's crazy
I go back
To the American football
Later I watch the moon
Rushing through cloud
And see her train
Crossing the Passage

COURTS

A party
At the tennis courts
Particles flying
Bodies swirling
She says "We're so close
Such friends"
Particles flying
Bodies swirling

I make the courts empty
The shelter-sheds silent
The gums just stirring
Dust   sometimes hit
In the cold light
Flying   swirling

SONG OF THE SECRET TRACKING

Hunt of mystery
Narrow track
Golden daisies
Gully walls
Legs   arms   chest
Know strange lightness
As they follow
Signs that whisper
"If you track
Not knowing why
The quarry
Will respond"

You will never know
Why you came
To tracking
Or why the quarry
Will respond
But you will
Be astounded
At the kill
That you hunt
And capture
And ingest
The providence
Self

TRANSCENDENT TRUCKS

We were driving trucks
Taking people here   there
We were in uniform
In a jungle
We were transporting
The people to safety
We were trying to – "transcend them"

On a road through jungle
We were whispering by a truck
Our backs to the canopy
Something emanated
We could feel it on our backs
We could feel the fear
An awful numbing
We wanted to get out
But I said "Stand
Stand and face it"

And it was watching us
Something dreadful
Because I woke
And I couldn't move
And the house was full of it
Full of fear and vines
The roaring of trucks
And a green mask
Shrieking

MEETING WITH ABORIGINAL ELDER CEDUNA 1985

We glanced as we spoke
Never staring
That consummate rudeness
So we glanced as we spoke
And with natural integrity
Began to know things
Without peering empirically
Or presuming
A positivist paradigm
Falsely measured
And paternally projected
And as we were talking
Suddenly we were Dreaming
Consciously Dreaming
Separate but collective
Unchanged but enhanced
Sufficiently demystified
And matter immeasurable

IT IS CERTAIN, PARMENIDES

Woken three times
Each time the moon
Has climbed further up
The bamboo slats

This fourth time
It has vanished
It is certain
Nothing has changed

TEA AT CAPE COUTTS

Ah   Lao Tse
Chuang Tse

No doubt you have
Been expecting me

How do you each
Have your tea

Ah   of course
The same   all three

ALEXANDRIA

Rising through the fading darkness
We found the eternal roofs of all things
And viewed   not like weathervane-
  philosophers
The preachers of prevailing winds
But as the teachers of change
Sister and brother   lovers   Helen
We observed the crucible
Of the secret chemistry of matter
Witnessed the lighting
Of the nerves   blood and limbs of life
Burned all clothes of mind and body
In the conscious flame of revelation
And naked mystics   again withdrew
To the lost library of vision and creation
Questioned the catalogues for ourselves
And argued with God

VISION AS JULIAN OF NORWICH

Ultimately the mind bares stars,
Having clarified into space.
And it approaches a guide,
Whose eyes are galaxies,
Whose face is destiny,
Who cautions, "Think atavistically,"
Who says simply, and clearly,
"You were born of stars
Whose maker watches
Their struggle and work,
Wonderfully domestic."
Ultimately the guide shows
That in the great home
Parental eyes are the stars,
And their children.
"And all shall be well,
But all shall be well,
And all manner of things
Shall be well."

VISION OF KINDERGARTEN
AND CONSTANTINE

In the many windowed basement
Kindergarten chairs
Alternate red   blue   yellow
Along the walls
I read with a teacher
Light flooding her desk
Removed in an alcove
Off a long room

In the many windowed palace
Banner bedecked pillars
Alternate red   blue   yellow
And so on the walls
I talk with Constantine
Light flooding his table
Removed in an apse
Off a great hall

MEISTER ECKHART
AT CAPE COUTTS

"In the seeing rather than being"

With the lights on
I reflect in the glass

With the lights off
The Passage flows

Staring down
I see further

I see further
And then deeper

Until I perceive
My blood's light

In its silence
Sits a monk

He stares at me

PHANTOM

Do you know me
I am here
You are there
In the theatre

Can you hear me
Or just sound
Waves across dimensions
My source faint
My meaning obscure
As it enters you

Can you see me
Or just light
Waves across dimensions
My source dim
My meaning vague
As it enters you

Do you pause
Lift your head
Think "What?"
And then don't

EARTH

Smelled the earth today
Walking up the overcast track
That dank   humus mushroom
That first arrests the man
And then the mortal

EARTHLING

From the earth
I delight in walking on it
I exalt in jumping above it
Sometimes I am
An earth-blown bubble
Which floats high
And sees everything

And I like to cheek
Like a blue wren
Earth and darkness and death
I'll be caught
But I walk
And jump and float and cheek
And know everything

URN

I slept with an earthen urn
Her flesh was cold and brown
Her hips were wide and hard
Her lips were dry and round

I held her close in the night
To love her and caress
Sleepy hands though searching
Could find no warm ingress

When I woke the urn was gone
My body moist like clay
I knew that it would find
An earthen womb one day

THE SKULL

In the night
Pissing in the pan
I spat white spittle
It formed like a skull
And stared up at me
Death imminent?
I thought   half consciously
The naked cold embracing me
I pissed on it
Pissed on and on
Pitilessly

I FOUND MY OWN SKULL

I found my own skull
The grey-white shell
Where I lived

Eye to socket
Emptiness

Ear to shell

Ocean

PREY

Suddenly
Under grey day
A great gum
Thrashed grey tentacles

For a frozen moment
In the streaming current
I was prey

MORTAL

Down here alone
Linked by lungs
To the air
By feet
To the earth
A suit of skin
Divides terror
From Ocean

BENEATH THE GAME

Thirteen skeletons are playing cricket
Under a bone sky of ribbed red cloud
Ten thousand skeletons sit
A charging skeleton bowls an x-ray
And skeletal stumps rattle
And eleven skeletons rattle
And ten thousand skeletons rattle
And a skeleton in black trousers condemns
And a lone and scoreless skeleton jerks
To a windy and skeletal stand
Bone of The Tree impotent
In one skill-less skeletal hand

REPTILIAN RETURN

On the shore
Skin flakes

Flesh peels
Skeleton dissolves

Spinal cord
Lashes back

Into Ocean

ADVERTISEMENT PLACED BY
TYRANNOSAURUS REXY

For two nights
I let the moon
Flood into my eyes
And all the third day
There had been
A rushing of thighs
Close up in my mind
On the third night
Again I let the moon
Flood in and flow
To where it might
With yellow waters
Re-hydrate forgotten things

Rex arrived
Just drifted up
Drifted   it seemed
From my heart and neck
Drifted up like a vision
Rex is my bottom line
You   don't get past Rex
Don't ever try   to get past Rexy
He keeps me fed
Eats rivals   anyone
He just – reacts
He can't think
So I do that for him

But I let him loose   often
It seems we're healthier that way
Anyway   to the point
Rexy wants to meet a Regina
For dining out
And fleshy times
Anyone out there
Got a Regina?

DARK WORLD

The dark gates'
Urgent close
Is sphincter swift
When sun-thoughts shaft
Through alien moods
Subsiding in
A putrid flood

Internal sun
Pour on the
Thick ebbing
Splashes of light
Chase back the blackness
Weld shut the gates
Of darkness
Those spread iron leaves
Defecating bruised
And grey blood
From wars raging
In the dark world

NOUN-GOD

Walking
Thinking
My use of
The noun God
Seems facile
Archaic
Every jeer of reason
Says primitive   religious
Every horror of event
Sneers fool
Noun-God
I feel foolish
Primitive

Sitting
Musing
I remember moments
When Noun-God
Is obvious
Is grace
When Noun-God
Reveals as vision
And I go
And return
Realised
Confirmed

Lying
Resolving
I'll keep Noun-God
Someone else
Might walk   sit   lie
Along my lines
Find where I go
Return   and smile
Like a noun-primitive
Noun-fool
Having been where
There is no parsing

DADDY AND MUMMY AND ME

Sun
SunSun
SunSunSun
SunSun
Sun

SeaSeaSeaSeaSeaSeaSeaSeaSeaSeaSeaSeaSeaSeaSeaSea
SeaSeaSeaSeaSeaSeaSeaSeaSeaSeaSeaSeaSeaSeaSeaSea
SeaSeaSeaSeaSeaSeaSeaSeaSeaSeaSeaSeaSeaSeaSeaSea
SeaSeaSeaSeaSeaSeaSeaSeaSeaSeaSeaSeaSeaSeaSeaSea
SeaSeaSeaSeaSeaSeaSeaSeaSeaSeaSeaSeaSeaSeaSeaSea
SeaSeaSeaSeaSeaSeaSeaSeaSeaSeaSeaSeaSeaSeaSeaSea
SeaSeaSeaSeaSeaSeaSeaSeaSeaSeaSeaSeaSeaSeaSeaSea
SeaSeaSeaSeaSeaSeaSeaSeaSeaSeaSeaSeaSeaSeaSeaSea
SeaSeaSeaSeaSeaSeaSeaSeaSeaSeaSeaSeaSeaSeaSeaSea

me

He took the sun for his father
And the sea for his mother
Was reborn a mystic-child
And lived happily ever after

REMEMBER MYSTERY THE ONLY SANCTUARY

The streets are sunny
And I'm walking today
Through the light
And shadow play
I want to throw my clothes away
I want to throw my clothes away
I want to walk
Through the sunny streets
Having thrown my clothes away

I'm walking
Through the sunny streets
Through the light
And shadow play
I want to throw my body away
I want to throw my body away
I want to walk
Through the sunny streets
Having thrown my body away

I'm walking
Through the sunny streets
Through the light
And shadow play
I have thrown my clothes away
I have thrown my body away
I am sunny streets
I am sunny day
I am light
And shadow play
Walk with me one day
Throw your clothes and body away